Trade Your Journey

Dedication

Normally this is dedicated to someone or something, not this time. I'm going to say this, it takes dedication from you to learn and develop as a trader and only you can make the decision to buy or sell. Only you can create a trading system that constantly performs with profits and education is the key.

This book is only a basic start guide; your real journey will begin after you have read this book cover to cover, researched, read, developed a trading system and educated yourself. I wanted to make this book short and keep the basics at low level.

Trading can be complex; this book will show you how I got started and how I organised myself. Hopefully you can take away something of use and I hope you enjoy the read.

This book is a basic start guide; it is not a get rich quick book. It will NOT teach you how to trade or make/earn money. What it will do is give you a great starting point.

Table of Contents

Trade Your Journey

A basic start guide

William Banks
5/21/2019

To start trading Forex or other options while never even touching platforms or seen charts before this basic guide will get you started. It will also be fun!

Trading Your Journey

Introduction

Let me introduce myself, my name is William Banks and I have been demo/live trading for 2 years now. What attracted me to trading was at the time you could start trading with little amount of money and make money from it, maybe even be debt free in 5 years. Little did I know?

I knew there was a mountain to climb, a long road to walk and oceans to cross before I could say with any certainty that I have enough skills to start live trading and knew that would be the start. This book hopefully will get you to the starting blocks with a little more knowledge and I hope some gems and insight you find valuable for the future.

I know when I started looking at the success stories and amounts people are making over different media sources like Facebook, Twitter and Instagram even you will say, this sounds easy, well they come across that way. In reality these amazing people that make X amount everyday or every week what they don't say is, it's taken them years of developing to get there. One guy I know took 7 years of developing his system to give mostly profits out before he made the complete switch over to trading life, that means he was making enough profit that matched his earning yearly and some. It all depends on your goals and how determined you are to learn and have a great trading plan.

You might not like this word Education but it's a key factor in your development to become a trader and you will find it addictive, fun and get sucked hook line and sinker into the world of money (sorry trading). Every body's favourite subject is money, some people don't like to admit it but you get a couple of guys together and start talking about cash, money, pay days and trading there goes most of the night.

Education is your friend, even today when I live trade or demo trade I include education into my routines every week and attend as many live webinars I can get my hands on. I watch YouTube videos and read forums; the list goes on and on. Your education can start at any time but will never end. Sometimes I found it helpful to revisit concepts to re-inform my knowledge and I make notes, taking notes is also a must. Plus I found re reading my notes really helps me get new concepts and others I've covered set in.

This is why I have dedicated sections to taking notes, recording, chart analysis, before and after trade analysis, back tests and all the information from your education you find useful. What I'm describing here is your Trading Journal. You will find on the Internet many people who will say it's the most important part of trading; you might talk to a friend who says it's important but does not do it. Please don't fall fowl of your mates philosophy, keeping a journal helps you to track your progress and you can revisit your journal any time and you should do this as often as you can. In the next chapter I give solutions on how to start one and give examples of data I've stored, so many platforms offer different things and again it's on you to choose which one suits you.

What is trading?

To put this in a nutshell, it's the process of buying or selling a product in the hope it goes down or up. When you sell or buy it back to market you take the difference as profit. It's that simple but hold on to your horses there cowboy.

You must learn how to and the many different ways you can spot the right trade opportunities to give you the goal, profits.

I'm also going to say this, what is trading, question, deserves a complete book in its own right and there are books dedicated to explaining this.

Some of you might be wondering right now why have a section about trading and not describe the trading process to us, well my trading methodology is to ask myself questions and when all those questions have the right answer I decide what to do next.

When first starting out and not ever touched a trading platform or software before this can seem like climbing a mountain, trust me I've been doing this for about 2 years now on demo accounts and live trading, I'm still teaching myself the market changes and you need to learn how to adapt with it.

What is the market? Well in a nutshell it's Forex, commodities, stocks, indices and cryptocurrencies these are the many different products you can buy or sell. During this book I won't touch on options, stocks, indices, commodities, cryptocurrencies or any other type of trading option out there because this book is for the complete beginner, I will focus on Forex trading. In fact I'm a Forex trader at heart but have dabbled in oil, gold, silver, coffee, sugar, gas and the lower spread indices. This book is not the Holy Grail and will not make you rich or even make you profits, that's on you. Only you can press the button, only you can decide to buy or sell, only you can design and develop your system and if you win give yourself a pat on the back, if you lose look in the mirror.

Trading can be heart bumping and other times it can be like watching snails move. The trick here is to have the right mind set we call this trading psychology, again there are books dedicated to this subject but here in this book I hope to give you a starting point and hopefully give you the ability to start your trading journey.

I'm not a professional trader my classification is a retail trader; this depends on how much capital you intend to start with and now due to rules past in 2018 you have to apply for a different status. What does this mean? Don't worry I go in detail on this when you are ready to go live.
Right now you should read through this book front to back and all will become clearer.

What's it like to win? Or what's it like to lose? These two questions can only be answered by you; this is based on your trading psychology. In my mind if I lose it hurts, it should do you've just lost money, my trading system gave me the right signals to trade and then the market flipped against me. I take those opportunities to learn, I will show you later how I analyse losing trades. If I win, I punch the sky and say yeah my system works, pat myself on the back and also analyse all winning trades, I will show you later how I do this.

There are traders who might tell you that what I'm doing is wrong, only you can decide this. Don't believe anybody or even me, there are no right or wrong answers in trading, form your own ideas, develop your own questions and feel any way you wish. Do you know why I say this? It's because at the end of the day only you can press that button and if it goes against you, nobody can be at blame. Trust in yourself and your system.

Where to start?

Like I said in the introduction I started by researching the web, reading, watching videos and asking questions on forums. It was from this two week period my friend highly recommended Baby pips website and now I'm saying this to you. I felt like writing a book with newbie's in mind, nobody recommended any books when I first started and while writing this book I kept that feeling I was going through not knowing anything.

It is for that reason that I wanted to create book giving you a great starting point, trading can be hair pulling and jumping for joy moments. We all start somewhere and the following chapters will give you an insight into my journey and hopefully once you read this book all the way through, it should give the heads up and you won't be feeling lost at the start.

How to use Baby Pips?

Basically sign up for an account the normal way, password, email and user name etc.......
Roll over or click education and start school of pipsology. Take your time and start at course 1, when you read everything on that lesson and have scrolled all the way to the bottom of page, you will be able to track your progress yes/no by clicking yes. Once you understand everything inside that concept being explained.

I highly recommend that you read it twice, once to get an understanding and the second time for notes, I had a wire hard covered bound A4 notebook at hand ready to takes notes on things I thought would be and sound important to remember.

You might get board or lose the willingness to continue like I did, so to get round this I started to watch YouTube videos and created a playlist for future reference, doing this broke up the reading and note taking. After about an hour or so watching trading videos and relaxing I was ready to learn some more. I also found it helpful to listen to music to block out outside noises while I read. I know what you are saying right now, can I have access to your playlist please? I'm going say no because it's on you to discover and dig out those gems of information. It's your journey, your trading, your research, your development and at the end of the day you pressing buy or sell.

When you finish the education on Babypips it has tools and a forum you can use, I highly recommend you take advantage of this when you first start trading because on the website there is a community section, a great place to learn, interact, post, ask questions and answer if you are feeling brave.

One more thing open a demo account with a broker of your choice, I used FXPRO because I did my broker research and chose them.
In baby pips they have an education lesson on choosing a broker, read it, read it and read it again. You might try a range of demo accounts from brokers just to get a feel of their platforms and software. I myself found the MT4 platform more appealing and most brokers offer MT4. I know what you are saying right now, what the hell is MT4? Baby pips describe opening an account and using MT4 in one of their lessons.

www.babypips.com

Your trading plan

I could have put my goals and what I wrote in my plan in this book but that would be wrong to do that, why? Because it's your trading plan that needs creating and everybody is different and wants different things. So what's in a trading plan, you might have your goals like I want to buy a lambo, retired at age 50, buy a castle and many others. Be realistic on goal setting and keep it on subject, that's the correct way.

Example of goals in trading you might set yourself
- I will only risk 1% of my account per trade
- I want to gain 2% on every trade win, day or week
- The minimum I want to make a week is 5%
- The maximum I want to make a week is 10% but more is welcome
- If I lose 4% in a day, I will stop trading and that's my limit
- I will not trade in high impact news events or when reports come out
- I will keep a trading journal/trading diary
- I will build several trading systems and test them out only on demo accounts
- I will factor in sometime in a day/week to do my trading education
- I will do analysis before placing a trade and on finished trades

Etc etc.................

You might find yourself breaking these up into life goals, general goals and the others into trading goals whatever floats your boat it is your trading plan after all. Babypips describe a trading plan very well and most sites will show something similar, research trading plans on YouTube and you will be overwhelmed with helpful advice on what to include and how to create one, but at the end of the day only you can decide the right direction.

Your trading plan can be thought of an interconnecting web of thought and processes, what I mean by this statement is it's a combination of parts that cross each other and you can't have one without the other, just like a trading system the beef of a trading plan.

Opening a trading demo account
This is the simplest thing you will do, all you need is a secure email address to use and create a password. Some platforms or brokers will ask you to create an account with them first, what that means is that you can login to their online website and have full control over the trading demo accounts you will create within your dashboard.

FXPRO will ask you to create an account first with them, once you have an account and logged in you can create a demo account and chose your platform, of course chose MT4 and you will be able to choose your leverage.

What's leverage? It's the amount of money your broker is prepared to lend you to buy or sell a product based on account size and this affects your used margin/margin level too.

Read and do Babypips they will give you more detailed description. In my view when first starting out you might want to chose 1/100 or 1/200 this will aid you and not restrict you when placing trades, for instance if you wanted to open a live account with a starting figure of 500 GBP then you would be under the classification of a retail trader and your leverage would be 1/30.

When I first started live trading I had 1/200 and it was good, now the EU and other governing bodies have brought in new rules to help people not lose all their money and you have to request from your broker to be placed under a professional status to give you 1/200 or something similar. Some brokers won't do this if you don't open with 2000GBP or have this amount in the account.

16

When you create a demo trading account you are given a Login number or name and a password for the account, it might also give you reference to which server to chose within the platform, once you've downloaded MT4 package to your desktop, launch the platform.

Screenshot of what yours might look like, this is my Think Markets demo account....

Click file and then chose Login to trade account another box will pop up....
Screenshot of box below

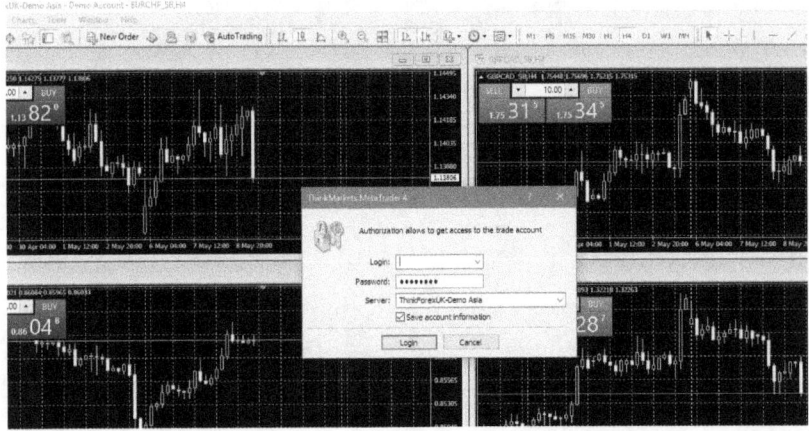

Enter your details and choose your correct server, yes you could check save account information this will save you re-entering this every time you want to trade.
When I switch between demo accounts or live ones I will have to re-enter anyways, but when you are first starting out and finding your feet one demo account is enough and having this checked will save time. Is it secure? So far in my journey it's been safe to do so.

That's it once you've logged in and you see your account number at the top of screen, you can play with MT4 and discover what buttons do what and don't worry about breaking it, have a go, press everything, if you do manage to break it, doubt that will happen you can just uninstall it and repeat the process. Ask yourself questions, develop and research on YouTube on how to use MT4 there's plenty of great videos on this subject. Don't forget take notes and add them to your trading journal.

Creating a trading system?

Below is a basic chart with no indicators, I have however styled my chart with colours and chose candles as my chart style. You might like to use bar chart or even a line style to present the price movements. The reason why I use candles is because it's easier (he say's) to spot candle patterns and turning points maybe price reversals. Never say yeah that's that candle type or pattern I'm buying or selling, you've just fallen into the trap of being over confidant with your candle analysis. This is why we build ourselves a trading system and backtest it, more on this later. For now a trading system has many building blocks, questions and I will show how I build mine and answer the many questions each might throw up.

A chart can be that simple like the one below, just build your trading rules and triggers to buy and sell, move onto backtesting to see if you would have won every trade. Trade on demo account and prove your system works, I reckon about a month to 6 months that should do it. Some people have even taken two years or more to prove the system works. What I show you in the section below is how to create a system and the process I went through with every system I have created since starting.

Top rule, take your time and don't rush to get it to live money, prove your system works over time, keep data and stats of every trade so that at the weekends when the market is doing nothing, this gives you the opportunity to take stock and do analysis on the trades, write up on all the factors. This is basically keeping a trading journal for which is highly recommended.

8 blocks in total here to create this trading system, but you might reduce these or even add more.

Let's get creative!!!!!!

Block 1: How to create a signal strategy

A signal strategy is something you develop over time to give you the signals to enter a trade via one click trading buy or sell or place a pending order. It could contain a series of indicators or you might choose to trade only the price itself, waiting for the price to hit key levels based on passed resistance or support levels. To be honest it's up to you, after visiting many websites, reading, watching videos and doing baby pips and many others you will have formed your own style.

I look at it like this, I ask myself questions and if those questions come back with yes, yes, and yes I trade. I'm not going to give you my signal strategy for one reason, if I lose then only I am to blame, that is the right frame of mind to get into. Don't copy strategies and don't just wack on as many indicators as you can, thinking it will give you the edge.

Develop reasoning; ask yourself I'm adding a moving average because? I'm adding a RSI because? and so on. Come up with rules for a buy trade and sell trade. Then with reasoning and a developed signal strategy you can move onto back testing. Only then you can see if your rules match up and if your whole signal strategy would produce winning trades.

Later I will also go into detail on how I back test a new signal strategy, for now read each section on creating a signal strategy. Below is an example of a signal strategy.

Example name - Spaceboy. I like to give my strategies a funky name and save it has a template within MT4 trader. This strategy is not a winning strategy nor is it losing, the only purpose is for education.

Below is the details of the spaceboy setup.

SIGNAL 1 - Bollinger Band Setting = Period 20, Shift 0, Dev 2, Apply to close, Colour red, thin line.
SIGNAL 2 - Stochastic Settings = %K Period 10, Slowing 3, %D Period 3, Price field Low/high, MA Method Simple.
SIGNAL 3 - RSI Settings = Period 10, Apply to close.

We will for the purpose of these examples and throughout the book are using this strategy all the way through for our signals to buy or sell, only for education purposes. As you read on you will get to see how we back test this strategy and how it produces signals.

One more thing to remember when designing or coming up with your strategy is keep it simple and have clear reasons why you include indicators on your charts, once you develop a simple to follow strategy and stick to it like clue, your trading will improve. Don't get disheartened when you lose because you will lose and your signal strategy is not perfect and will never be perfect.
Move onto the buy or sell strategy and rules?

Block 2: Buy and sell strategy

Having a clear idea and set rules for buying and selling will enforce your system, these rules will depend on your signal strategy and of course your trade rules. You might find it helpful to write these rules down in a note book and have that open page ready sitting at the terminal. Once you've got these rules imprinted into your mind there will be no need to have them in front of you, but at the early stages of developing your system and rules you will be changing them more often. This page will change overtime; it has to, the market changes so you do to.

You might be saying what's the point in writing a rules page if the rules over time will have to change? I say this because the market does change and when I say change the rules, I mean minor tweaks.

For example: You start trading only on the hourly time frame, one of your rules says check the 30min chart and if the price is above the top band and curving up then buy.

Later after many trades losing or winning you decide to change this rule to, the same as before but count two candles that close above the top band then buy on the hourly chart.

Buy or Sell rules based on Spaceboy's signal strategy

The rules below are independent of each other and if one rule fits trade it. These are very simple rules and you could use candle analysis and drawing tools in combination with these, also use a little bit of patience before hitting the trade button. What is a reactive rule? I called it this because candles are reactive to price change and most often or not based on how this system performed over the years the rule stands to be true most of the time. But again things change the market changes. Also I'm following Bollinger band rules like you should.

What is continuation rule? Well it's simply following the trend, most trends within bands start to curve upwards or downwards signalling a new trend starting, based on charts and back testing, if we had two candles that close above the top band this is an upward trend starting in my view, so we will buy based on our trade rules and the same goes for the sell side. The rule of two candles closing just described is one that I made up for this system, it might work or it might not, you could wait for just one candle or even three candles to close above or below. It's up to you!

Rules for Spaceboy system below.

Buy Rule 1: A reactive rule
IF... the body of the active candle has closed above middle band
AND... RSI is above the 50% Line
AND... Stochastic main line above the 50% Line

Buy Rule 2: Continuation rule
IF... two candles have closed above the top band
AND... RSI is above the 50% Line
AND... Stochastic main line above the 50% Line

Sell Rule 1: A reactive rule
IF... the body of the active candle has closed below middle band
AND... RSI is below the 50% Line
AND... Stochastic main line below the 50% Line

Sell Rule 2: Continuation rule
IF... two candles have closed below the bottom band
AND... RSI is below the 50% Line
AND... Stochastic main line below the 50% Line

When Not to buy!
IF... the candle has closed above the middle band and closed above top band also, basically one big candle
You will be waiting for the second candle to close above the top band that would meet the buy rule 2.
Don't buy if you see just the wick of the candle poking through the middle band, it has to be the body to meet buy rule 1.

When Not to sell!
IF... the candle has closed below the middle band and closed below bottom band also, basically one big candle
You will be waiting for the second candle to close below the bottom band that would meet the sell rule 2.

Don't sell if you see just the wick of the candle poking through the middle band, it has to be the body to meet sell rule 1.

Overview

These rules above are just a starting point; they will need tweaking and adjusting. You might even create and add more rules or indicators to the chart to filter out wrong decisions, but at the end of the day it's up to you. Your system you create must have rules for buying and selling, remember I mentioned having your rules written down on a piece of paper alongside your computer while trading, so we have two rules each for buy and sell.
Yours will be based on your system. If you add more rules you will need to include them on this page or remember them.

Now that we have a signal strategy and rules to trade we can move onto backtesting, it is through backtesting we develop our stop loss and take profit strategies.

Block 3: Backtesting

I'm going to assume you have had a little play around with MT4 trader platform and know how to do the basics, if not there is plenty of YouTube videos and websites who offer tutorials on this. Again this book would of been huge undertaking to include everything but the kitchen sink and there are books dedicated to teaching MT4 trader platform. I myself used YouTube, websites and a lot of discovery inside a demo account to fully understand how to use it and even today learn new things.

All traders approach the topic of backtesting in different ways, this is how I backtest because I believe it gives me the right answers, you on the other hand might take from this and add more to it. Like I said from the start it's your journey, your trading, your processing and You pressing the button. You have to form your own rationale around the system you create.

Let's get backtesting!!!

You might hear many people say I've back tested the system and it looks promising. What does backtesting mean? Well we have just created a new system with signals and rules for trading. We need some way of testing this system to see if our rules produce correct predictions or profit per trade, we could test our system in a demo account and just trade it straight off the bat with live data coming through to us and do it that way.
Or we could back test it while doing something called paper trading on past historical data trading.

From this we will be able to set down our stop loss and take profit targets and see if our system really works. I highly recommend this way of doing things because using the tools MT4 provide like the crosshair we can see firsthand if entering a trade based on our rules if we would have made profits. Plus if we said stop loss at 200 and take profit at 300 would we win every trade, can we add to the take profit side and maximize our gain, maybe we need to add to the stop loss. All these questions will be answered while backtesting.

Where to start/setup on eurusd H1 chart

1. Place all three indicators on the chart
2. Find a candle formation or setup that matches our rules for ether buy or sell
3. Draw a horizontal line where we would of entered the trade, the open of the new candle
4. Draw a vertical line on the candle you would of entered on
5. Use the crosshair and get a reference value to where 200 stop loss and 300 take profit lines should be, write these numbers down on a piece of paper so that you can now draw two horizontal lines for SL and TP targets. You might need to flip to a higher time frame to be able to get the values and draw the lines
6. Draw a rectangle or square from the entry to the take profit line, do the same for the stop loss, colour each square light pink or red for the stop loss section and green for take profit section. You could draw the rectangles with the same width that helps, also when you draw them on the chart you have a choice to draw the shape in the background, I would because it helps me visualize the trade better and the candles overlay over the shapes
7. Delete the lines from step 5

You have everything on the chart now to start backtesting, you may need to adjust a few things because I'm not sitting there with you and don't know if you've picked the right candle colours or chart setting. You might prefer to change the chart setting into black and white while you backtest, it help me to get started and now it's second nature, you can save each chart style as a template eg.. Spaceboy, Spaceboy_BW and maybe Spaceboy_Print. Switching between these can be time saving.

Let's do analysis on the first trade by paper trading.

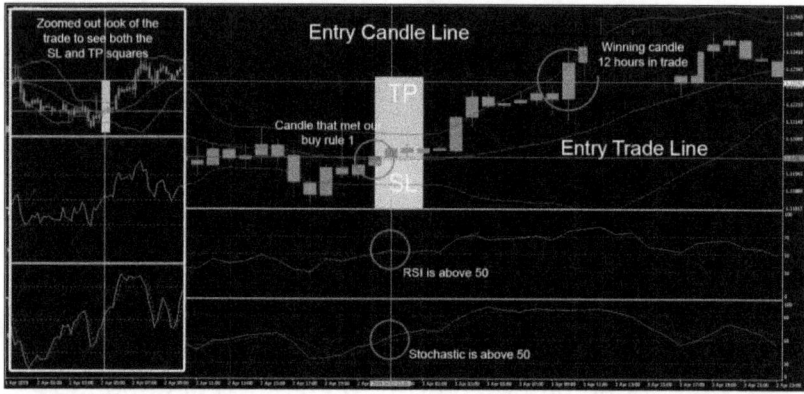

Remember me saying about black and white chart setting, then below is the same trade with drawing

As you can see the first trade opportunity was not hard to find, the key in backtesting is to be honest. Now you won't need to screen capture every trade and write stuff on it, you can if you want to, all you will need to do is set up your squares based on the 7 steps above. Once this is done all you need to do is move the entry line to the next buy or sell opportunity, drag the SL and TP squares across and see if that was a winner. I always keep a note book aside and write down details of every trade plus keep a tally of losing/winning trades.

It's up to you how many you test, some people recommend doing 100, 50 or 25 tests, again it's your system and getting it right can mean the difference between losing and winning. You could create a spread sheet and add data into that, my suggestion is to create a different sheet per setting, these settings above are SL=200 TP=300 and it's through backtesting we can see if the level values are going to produce more winning trades.

Doing these tests give us the opportunity to write our trade rules, take profit strategy, stop loss strategy, end trade strategy and cancel trade strategy based on our system. These rules you can think of as how we will finish the trade.

Block 4: Trade rules

These rules below are based on my own circumstances and yours might need changing to suit you. There are two sets of rules in my view, the ones that cover general settings and the other set that covers the trade itself. Also the values given here are based on backtesting the system and completing months of learning.

General setting:

1. For our system trading starts at 8 am, London open
2. Trade only on the hourly time frame
3. One click trading/direct execution
4. Right click order and modify order to set stop loss and take profit levels
5. Volume traded is based on leverage
6. Only trade 1% risk of account in volume size
7. Cannot exceed half of my available free margin
8. The spread cannot be greater than 3
9. No trading past 4 pm, London close
10. Will only trade EURUSD

Trade rules:

1. **Volume = 0.01**, but can vary based on account size
2. **Stop loss = 200** Points, will need to vary over time due to market conditions
3. **Take profit = 300** Points, will need to vary over time due to market conditions

Block 5: Take profit strategy

Now that we have done backtesting we can see setting our take profit at 300 could be a good start, I base it on the number of wins over losing trades. If it always hit TP then you could have retested with 400 targets or reduced it to 250. That's the purpose of backtesting finding and tweaking the strategy to give the best results, using the crosshair and other tools while backtesting will improve your decision making and improve the systems rules and you might have to rewrite the rules and add to them.

Coming up with one take profit strategy could work most of the time, but I like to come with other options. These options might include:

1. Let the price or candle hit TP target
2. Wait for the price get close to the TP, place a Trailing Stop on and drag TP well out of the way. Wait for the price to keep dragging the SL banking money, then cancel out on SL by itself
3. Don't place a TP, wait for a target price to build in profits then place a Trailing Stop
4. Cancel the trade once it hits a target, we would not be placing a TP or TS

Developing a Take Profit strategy based on Fibonacci levels, candle analysis, price movement or even support and resistance is going deep into trading knowledge, this takes time to discover. The purpose of the book is to get you on the road trading Forex, trading in general and while you are still learning off your own back trade only on demo accounts. I will say this YouTube is a great source of information and finding answers there is not hard to do.

If you do set a TP level I have a couple of rules, set it slightly above your SL level, so we have a SL=200 for our system, so our TP=300 and based on backtesting I'm getting positive results. Those levels can be adjusted at any time to suit our test trading environment (demo account) or backtesting results. Another rule is have a very good reason why you are placing it at that level, based on my testing at 300 TP seemed to produce more wins than losses, when I changed it to 400 TP the results went down. So have a good reason why? Final rule, don't be greedy. In fact it's the most important rule of trading in whole; setting yourself realistic targets to start with will boost your trading. You will not become this super awesome trader or rich over night, think of your first steps into trading like sorting through grains of sand in a Petri dish with a pair of tweezers, long and tiresome.

Block 6: Stop loss strategy

The idea behind setting a Stop Loss is to prevent losing too much money and give your trade some breathing space because your system answered all the questions to trade that way and it whip sawed against you. If you didn't place a stop loss your account will soon become empty and end at zero, better known as a blown account.

While backtesting and using the crosshair on several trade opportunities, I saw based on my spaceboy system, setting the SL at 100 would produce more losing trades than winners, setting it at 200 more winners came out. Even this might need changing again once I place some demo trades on and I will encounter problems along the way, the rules will need updating to. A system and your system will be forever changing and you need to change with it, just before you do change or tweak it, give those setting and rules at least 100 demo trades placed before you say to yourself this system is crud I need to change something, that's why keeping a trading journal is the most important part on your trading discovery.

Thinking of losses or losing trades can be hard, but it's the most important thing in trading. Understand how trading volumes, margin used, free margin, leverage and account balance will dictate what your stop loss will be. If you want to risk more and give each trade a fighting chance or breathing room then you go for it. At the end of the day it's your trading journey you make the decisions.

Developing a Stop Loss strategy based on Fibonacci levels, candle analysis, price movement or even support and resistance is going deep into trading knowledge, this takes time to discover. The purpose of the book is to get you on the road trading Forex, trading in general and while you are still learning off your own back trade only on demo accounts. I will say this YouTube and the internet is a great source of information and finding answers on them is not hard to do.

Block 7: End trade strategy

You might think with a stop loss we won't need an end trade strategy, you would be wrong let me explain because we have many options to consider to preserve capital or add to it.

Options
1. The trade will end ether on TP or SL, in other words set it and leave it
2. The price might get close to your TP and by reading the stochastic, RSI, bands, candles or the Support/ Resistance you decide it's about to tank against you, cancel the trade manually and take profits
3. The price might get close to your SL and by reading the stochastic, RSI, bands, candles or the Support/ Resistance you decide it will never reverse your way, so you cancel the trade manually and take a loss
4. You've been watching news on TV and bad impact report has come out about the euro zone, you're on a buy eurusd, ummm! You say to yourself, it's tanking, heading downward slightly. You could hold or get out now with a little loss

5. When I first started I had a rule that when it's 9:30pm at night all trades would be cancelled weather in profit or loss, why? Because you would not incur swap fees and most brokers will tally up your account around 9:45 at night and then send you your daily report via email. Basically sleep well my friend.
6. You are in a trade buying eurusd, the finished candle meets buy rule 1 of our spaceboy system and closes above the middle band and the next candle closes just above the one we entered, the third closes below the middle band, ummmm! I wonder is this trade going south. We know it's in a tight range and our sell rule 1 has just been for filled. We could cancel the buy and now jump on a sell.

Whichever option you chose or add to the list it's up to you what you do next, that's why in my trading plan I have an end trade strategy and it's different per trading system I create. You will find once you start backtesting and demo trading your newly created system the options for all the above and details in all blocks might need adjusting, that's why I call it developing your system. It gives you an insight into the inner working of the system and produces data so that you can say with any confidence, this system is profitable.

Block 8: Placing a trade strategy

The spaceboy system uses one click execution and we place the SL and TP by right clicking the order and then click modify. We write our points in each of the boxes and click the button at the bottom inside the pop up window. If you have the last used option clicked, you can find this within tools menu, options and then the trade tab. This will be easier because when you right click the order and then click modify the SL and TP last used will be there ready.

Another placing a trade strategy might be, we could place a buy stop pending order just above the middle band and not wait for it to close above the middle band at all. We would base this buy stop on the last candle that did finish above the middle band. The same for sell option rules, we would be placing a sell stop just below the middle band and just below the last candle that did close below the middle band.

The whole process of placing a trade is open to you and can only be up to you. Every system you create will have a different approach maybe. That's why over the last two years I have created 10 or more systems and each have tailored ways of trading. You might develop a completely new system and you can only place pending orders or you might only place sell limit and buy limit pending orders on if you've developed a system that trades price ranges.

Overview creating your trading system

Wow! Creating a trading system was hard work and long to do, but fun dare I say. Now that we have it we can prove whether it works by demo trading it in a demo account. This is the long stuff and you might be doing this for months but all worth it and you will be changing aspects and rules in your trading system, trust me you will. This could be your potential winning system so take your time and get it right. All above rules and blocks are for the spaceboy system and it's written here in this book only for education purposes.

Keeping a trading journal

An important process you might like to try, other traders describe keeping a trading journal has more important than trading itself. Why? Because it's a way of you tracking your journey and progress as a trader. Having a record of trades, plans, goals, audio, systems, screenshots, rules, research, links, PDF's, docs and notes all in one place will help you in monitoring your trading journey.

There are several options in how you do this:
1. Physical version, you could keep an A4 arch file with tab separators for the different subjects or similar.
2. Online version, this is more eco friendly and if you pick the right platform, you can take your trading journal everywhere you go and add to it from any place any time.
3. Combination of two, when I take part in webinars and trade every day I like to keep a notebook handy. When I was learning in the first few months I kept an A4 wire bound hardback notebook as my journal, then when I found my feet started experimenting with online platforms to keep links, docs and trades etc...

What platforms have I used and why?

Trello

I use Trello mainly for keeping records of trades on demo accounts because it allows me to upload a screenshot of the trade and details per card. Once the trade is finished I can do some analysis on that trade and enter my thoughts and finding within that same trade card, making it easier to record progress. In fact I do have another board with lists and many cards on them with general research from around the web. You can attach YouTube videos, docs, notes, audio, pictures, links to docs, PDF's and much more.

Again it's up to you what you do with this platform; you could build a board per trading system and place everything to do with that system including rules on that board. The options are endless.

Another great feature of Trello is that you can print the whole board out on hard copy or PDF; you also can print any one list out. Why would this be good? Because let's say you keep a A4 arch file trading journal to track your progress and show people, this feature will be valuable. You might have joined a training program and have booked a one to one mentoring session he or she might want to see your progress, you take your laptop and phone but no signal, no WiFi, no internet, horror. No horror if you had it printed or saved as PDF from Trello.

There's a lot you can do with this application your mind knows no bounds and one more thing I need to say about Trello, let's say you and your friends all decide to study trading and develop yourselves as traders. Trello has a wonderful team option allowing you to create a team board and the whole team can add, edit, delete and comment on anything anywhere. Also let's say your mentor or friend wants to track your progress, you can simply invite them to join any board that will also give them the same rights as above. Weather you create a team board or just one personal board cross collaboration just got easier.

Evernote

I use Evernote mainly for keeping research from the web, if you get Chromes Evernote web clipper extension installed you will be able to collect all sorts of info with a simple click.
Another aspect I like about Evernote is that you can record your voice and attach that per entry, maybe you have attended a live training show or had a one to one training session with a mentor and recorded the speaker and you can attach that sound/audio file too.

The Evernote app for mobiles is another way for you to carry all your info with you, not only can to edit notes and add to them you can create new ones. Allowing you to do research on the bus, train, and plane or even waiting for an event. In fact I have a friend that uses Evernote to take notes while attending live trading events.

You have the ability to import notes from OneNote, let's say you try lots of platforms and chose this one as your favourite, Evernote allows import from OneNote under the file menu tab at the top. If you wanted to keep a hard copy of each of your notes then there is a print option, also print to PDF choice.

When you first start out on your trading journey combining learning and the process of learning all the new techniques can be overwhelming, just take it step by step and at your own pace. You could develop what's known as trader's burnout, I've had this at least 3 times. It's only having a trading journal and platforms like this I can monitor my progress and know that I'm on the right path.

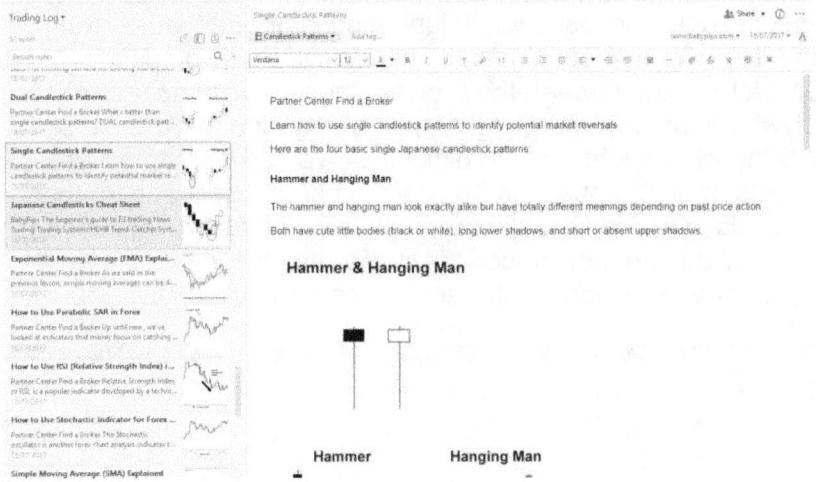

OneNote

At the start of my trading journey I used OneNote and an array of Microsoft software just because I've used them for university before and know the power of them. While writing this book I rediscovered OneNote and thought what I can say about it, so I did some digging around and played with the features it supports.

Wow! Glad I did. Now I might be converted and place all my journal entries into OneNote. My idea is to use all three platforms for different reasons. I consider OneNote as my online A4 arch file and the most important stuff that really matters to me and my trading will be placed within it, Trello will be my trade log and Evernote will be my dumping ground of thoughts and ideas.

Everything I have mentioned above can be done within OneNote including team collaboration by email invites and even printing or importing text/images direct from email sources into OneNote, but your trading journal should be personal and it's up to you if want to share and collaborate.

Now that I have rediscovered OneNote while writing this book I'm going be using it as my main hub, the place to go when I need to find research, videos, PDF's, note's, webpage articles, trade logs, trading systems, results and everything in between.

There is only one issue you might encounter and that's having access to your notebook across multi devices, if you used OneNote online through the browser then you can access it anywhere, but if you are using apps of any kind for Android or IOS then you might run into difficulty. If you do want to access the info through apps then Trello would be my best app for that, my thinking is I could collaborate on Trello and store info etc and then pull out the most important stuff to be placed into OneNote. I myself have a Windows phone and can access it anywhere.

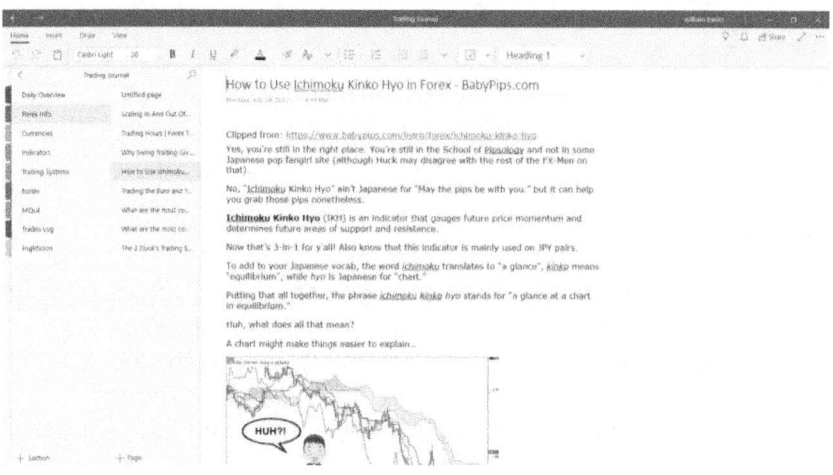

Overview on keeping journal software

When it comes to software to use there is no right solution that fits across the board, you might be using 2 or maybe 4 different platforms to get the job done. I have used and am using Google Sheets, Docs, Slides and Google Keep alongside these other platforms mentioned. I would like one solution but the advantage of using the ones I've mentioned is, they are all free. So I'm going to be using OneNote as my hub when I sit in front of the computer and do trading, learning and trade analysis. The other software can be used as a holding system before I copy relevant info from across the platforms I use and insert it into OneNote. If I need something, track progress or where can find this out, I will know where to find it inside OneNote.

Keeping a trading log

Some people see it as your trading journal but I look at it like this, a trading log is a list of trades you placed testing out your new system or live trades and you want to gauge your performance and performance of the system itself.

While writing out each trade entry you could have a thoughts section or how you feel column, this will give you an insight into your mental state when placing the trade. When the trade is over win or lose you could have a after trade thought and feel section, when you read these back and do analysis on the trade via the chart you have a better understanding of your system, your trading, mistakes, trading patterns and trading performance.

Your trading log in my view is another important part of trading your journey, this is where you will analyze all your trades and write up on them. Keeping a spread sheet of trades is the easy bit it's what you do with this information that counts. I talked about analysing winning or losing trades a bit ago, well a trading log book is where you will do this.

Software for trading logs and trade analysis

Two main programs I've used over my time for the trade entry are Microsoft Excel and Google Sheets, these are free and easy to use. As for analysis of trades I've used Trello, OneNote, Evernote and even Google keep.

My favourite is Trello for this purpose because you can comment, upload pictures, colour code each card and create more lists to help the process. One advantage of OneNote and Evernote over Trello is that laying out each trade within its own sheet or entry everything you type is on one sheet, more like a word doc and I've also found this very useful. It's up to you and it's only by trying the software out you can make an informed choice on which suits your style of recording your trade analysis.

Below of screenshots of trade log books from Excel and Google Sheets, not much difference and both do the same job. Again it's your choice which one you prefer to use, so give both a try. One thing to consider when choosing is whether you want to have access across multi devices to the data and maybe give access to it for your mentors, team, group or even trading partner.

Google Sheets

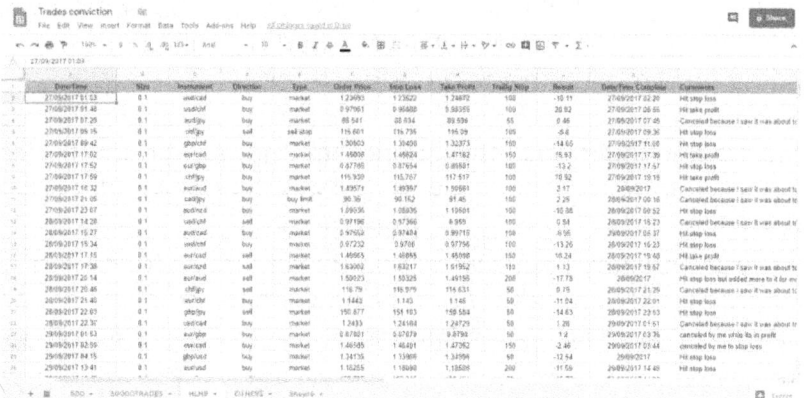

Microsoft excel

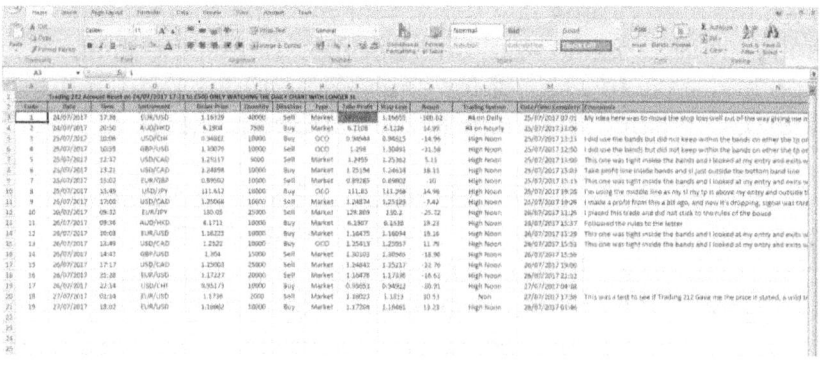

Trello to record trade analysis

For the purpose of showcasing each platform and the different styles each contain I will be placing a demo trade based on the SpaceBoy system, recording the trade and doing the after trade analysis. Let's start with Trello for trade analysis...

First create a list called live demo trades or you could call it Trades on/ Trades placed and add your first card to that list after you've placed the trade of course. Next take a screenshot from MT4 or other platform of the demo trade, normally this is done by right clicking the chart itself and selecting save as picture.

When you create a card in Trello and give it a name press enter this will create a new entry for that list, then just click that card to open up the editing side of the card where you can add images, text, videos and comment plus a whole host of other things.

The screenshot below has a colour label of orange because I don't yet know if it's going to be a winning (green) or losing (red) it's up to you if colour labelling is your thing, I also label it orange because I know just by looking at the colour labels if it's got a screenshot attached (orange), winning (green) or losing (red) and if I've done after trade analysis on that trade (blue).

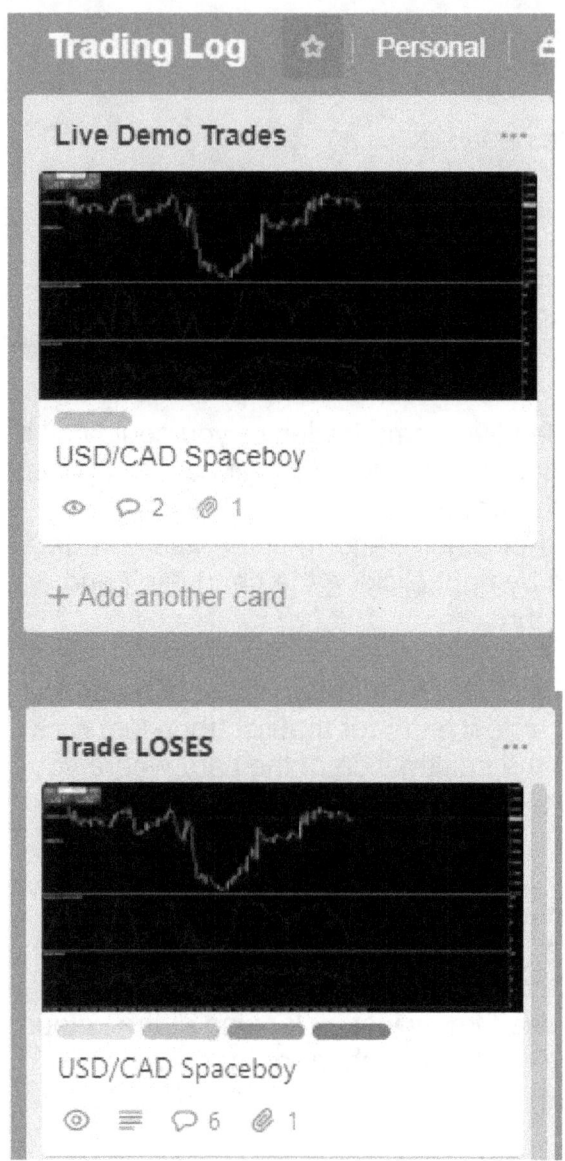

Live Demo Trades

USD/CAD Spaceboy

👁 💬 2 📎 1

+ Add another card

Trade LOSES

USD/CAD Spaceboy

👁 ≡ 💬 6 📎 1

OneNote to record trade analysis

OneNote has sections and then you had pages to them, so Spaceboy system has one page added USD/CAD a live demo trade which came out at a loss. One advantage over Trello is that in OneNote you can add everything into one page and this can scroll and scroll. You can add video, images, links, and text and even insert spread sheet data into the page. Best part about this if you were getting mentored you can share this Notebook with someone and they will be able to see what you entered and add comments on those notes.

You might create one page for losing trades and one for winning trades; you could also create a page for all those rules and setting. Below I have created one page for one trade and inserted two screenshots, you might decide to just to insert one image and text along the side. OneNote is very adaptable and customisable. Make it your own.

Evernote to record trade analysis

Very similar to OneNote but can be restrictive in the editing side and arrangement. But for a free platform it's got merits. Just like OneNote you can add video, text and images. You can also clip stuff from the internet, let's say you placed a trade and high impact news came out and your trade won or lost. You could find the news item via the internet website of choice and clip this to your page of analysis to show why your trade went the way it did, you can also do this with OneNote. Make it your own.

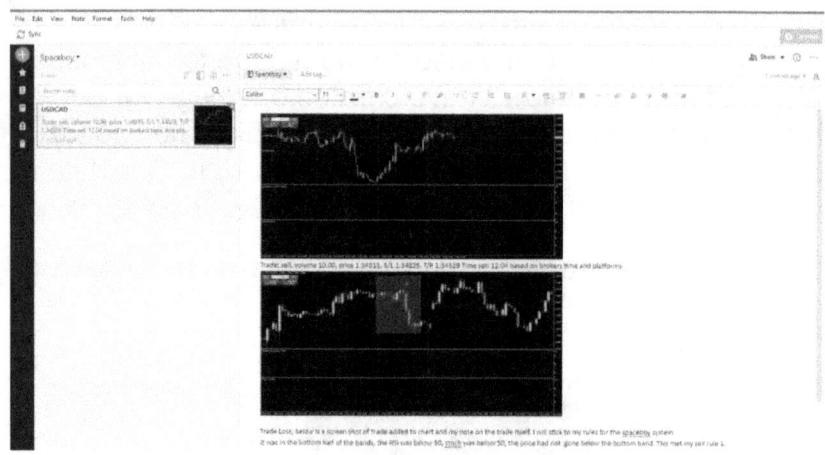

Before trade analysis and after

The techniques I showed you in backtesting section can be reused here, the before trade analysis is you following your signal strategy rules. If they match of course you will trade that way.

What do you do after the trade is finished? You can screenshot the chart before like I have said and after the trade is finished screenshot again. That way you can compare it and make notes on what worked or maybe changes to the system itself after you have traded at least 100 ++ trades. This process will develop and you will find your groove an easy way of reporting on your progress.

Some traders open the screenshot and edit it inside photo editing software packages, GIMP (Free) and Photoshop work well. I have also used on the odd occasion Microsoft paint. You are then able to draw and write all over it, the more you do this the more you can understand how effective your trading system will be.

Example of after trade drawing on chart

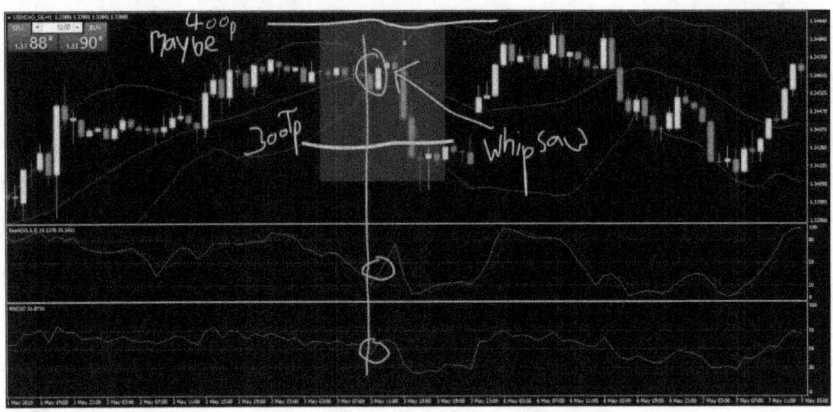

Positive and negative thoughts

OK we have a basic system together and it's not been tested much, we have placed a few trades and there has been losing and winning ones.

But how do cope with positive and negative thoughts during the trade?

Some questions might be, should I cancel the trade now with PL profit/Loss, should I leave it, economic news is bad and I'm buying I'll get out before I lose it, I've just lost and it was hitting resistance so it should bounce on that, I'll jump back on that pair, I believe by just looking at the chart it's going up, I've won 5 in a row and this looks good and many more.

How do I not feel lost and make stupid mistakes?

Simple stick to your trading system, if you have the rules set down then you can't be lost or even feel positive or negative. If you lose you will know you were following your system to the letter.

Your system might need tweaking but at least wait until you've placed 100 ++ trades and done analysis on the data.

One of the biggest problems in trading is your trading psychology; there are many books, websites and videos out there to discover. Like I said at the start of the book your mental state is key to keeping on track, that's why we develop a trading plan, trading system and keep a journal.

If you do feel burnt out and you will, close the laptop. Turn everything off and walk away for a week. Reread your trading journal and system rules. Make notes on your emotions before the trade, during the trade and after the trade. Go back and educate, doing these things will build your confidence and prepare you for the next bout of trading, but above all stick to the system rules and don't lose heart.

Watch lists

You might hear this term many times but not understand how to use or produce one. We for the purpose of the book developed the Spaceboy system, the rules are the rules and we must follow them.

Let's say we forget just trading eurusd and open around 10 pairs of currencies and we applied the Spaceboy system template to them all, we then do analysis on all 10 and decide four of the pairs have nearly met our rules, we create a watch list and add them to that.

You could decide to use pen and paper, sticky notes, notepad, create a new sheet within our trade log book called watch list or even open these four pairs inside a multi window view point inside MT4 ready to pounce and place a trade.

As you develop your skills, build systems and practise trading within demo accounts your choices will widen and trading style will shine through.

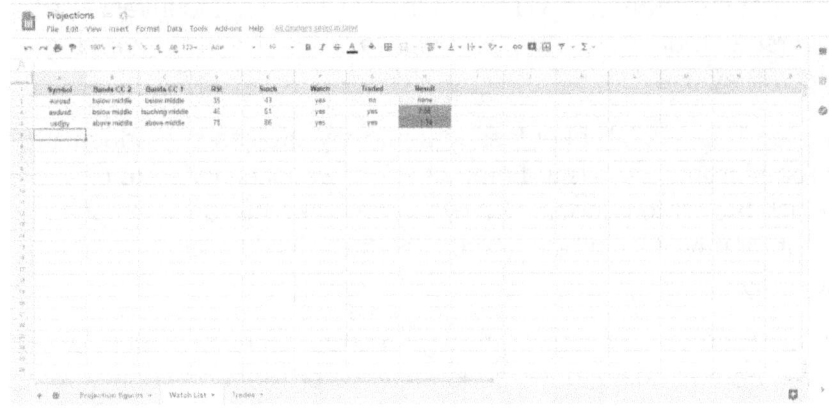

Before you go live

So you've been demo trading your systems for about 6 months ++ and you think you have a winning system, just before you bite the bullet and invest real money you might want to research brokers for a day or two.

When you first started out on your trading journey I'm assuming you opened as many demo accounts as possible with different brokers, in that process you could of traded with MT4, MT5 and designed apps from these brokers. It's while you are in this experiment stage you understand how these platforms perform and if they suit your needs, what this stage does not do is say whether these brokers are going to be right for you or even safe to do so.

That's where the British FCA Financial Conduct Authority will be your friend, if you have purchased this book in another country you will have to look up your countries equivalent governing body. Here you will be able you research the broker and find out if they are registered and any problems that company might have against their name, if you live in the UK and want to invest in an overseas broker then you will need to find out which governing body they use.

I used Baby pips broker lesson to aid my choices and education, I read forums and visited many trading websites trying to gauge which broker to choose. Only you can make this decision, it's your money, it's important and like I have said before it's your journey.

A quick note you might want to get sorted out before going live or even demo trading, get a good antivirus provider on your computer. That way, just in case scum bags out there won't be able to pinch your details or download toads or bugs on your computer. Just a thought and it's best to be prepared, this is standard stuff anyways for all computer needs. Be safe online people.

Conclusion

Hopefully you have read the book cover to cover and it's only taken a few hours. After all that you should be more confidant in starting baby pips, trading, learning and organising yourself to be disciplined in the process.

Your trading journey starts now, take your time and get it right, it is said 90% of new traders that open a real account have a blow out, in other words lose all their money, don't be part of that 90%. Be cool, wait for the best moment, follow your system and above all don't be greedy, know when to get in and know when to get out.

The trading system I developed for this book for education purposes only has 8 blocks that I described earlier, you should only take these as a guide, you can take away or even add more blocks, it's your trading journey you are making the decisions.

Just before the last words of the book, please read where to go from here, this is a check list that I completed when I started out and it helped me understand some concepts of trading. To be honest I'm still learning, building, developing and making mistakes.

Where to go from here
- Read and do Baby Pips
- Read, watch videos, visit websites and read books
- Setup demo account and Download MT4 or apps
- Organize and plan your trading journal
- Develop a trading plan
- Develop a trading system
- Demo trade your system
- Analyse your progress

Thank You

Wow! You are awesome you've taken the first steps in understanding where to start by reading this book. If the sale of the book is a success I plan to write another that goes in more detail and an in-depth look at using the MT4, other options for trading, trading apps and maybe touch on EA's electronic assistants.

Your trading journey starts Now!

www.ingramcontent.com/pod-product-compliance
Lightning Source LLC
Chambersburg PA
CBHW051204170526
45158CB00005B/1811